1 Introduction

Various studies emphasize the importance of variations in macroeconomic volatility to understand fluctuations in financial markets and the macroeconomy.[1] Bansal, Kiku, Shaliastovich, and Yaron (2012), Bali and Zhou (2012) and Campbell, Giglio, Polk, and Turley (2012) recently provided empirical evidence showing that compensation for volatility risk is important to understanding the cross-sectional variation in equity returns. In spite of the persuasive literature documenting the impact of aggregate macroeconomic volatility on asset prices, the literature has paid little attention to explaining the underlying determinants of a firm's compensation for volatility risk. To fill this gap, in this paper I propose a production-based asset pricing model and provide empirical evidence showing that compensation for volatility risk is closely related to a firm's reliance on skilled labor.

The production-based asset pricing model presented here extends the model of labor demand with non-convex adjustment costs of Bentolila and Bertola (1990), Caballero, Engel, and Haltiwanger (1997), and Cooper and Willis (2009) to allow for labor heterogeneity and two sources of macroeconomic risk. In my model, firms differ in their reliance on skilled labor, and they face linear adjustment costs in labor that are increasing with the skill of the worker. Also, firms face two sources of macroeconomic risk: fluctuations in aggregate productivity and time-varying volatility of productivity growth. The stochastic discount factor to compute the compensation for these risks, and asset prices in general, comes from the long-run risks model of Bansal and Yaron (2004). I use this model as a laboratory to simultaneously study the impact of fluctuations in aggregate volatility on a firm's labor demand and its cost of equity.

In the model, a rise in aggregate volatility slows a firm's labor demand reaction to changes

---

[1] Most notable papers include those by Kandel and Stambaugh (1990), which explores an equilibrium asset pricing model in which the mean and variance of consumption growth vary through time; Bansal and Yaron (2004), which asserts that long-run fluctuations in expected growth and long-run fluctuations in consumption volatility are important to explain asset prices; and Bekaert, Engstrom, and Xing (2009) which explores the importance of changes in the conditional variance of dividend growth and time-varying risk aversion in explaining asset markets. Bansal, Khatchatrian, and Yaron (2005), Bollerslev, Tauchen, and Zhou (2009), Bollerslev, Xu, and Zhou (2012), and Bansal, Kiku, and Yaron (2012) present empirical evidence showing that fluctuations in economic uncertainty impact asset valuations. Finally, Bloom, Floetotto, Jaimovich, Saporta-Eksten, and Terry (2012) and Bloom (2009) show that an increase in aggregate uncertainty lowers hiring and investment rates, as well as consumer durable expenditures. Justiniano and Primiceri (2008), Fernández-Villaverde, Guerrón-Quintana, Rubio-Ramirez, and Uribe (2009), and Fernández-Villaverde, Guerrón-Quintana, Kuester, and Rubio-Ramírez (2011) show that taking into account time-varying volatility is important to understand aggregate fluctuations as well as to undertake policy analysis.

in economic conditions, reducing its ability to smooth cash flows. Firms with a high share of skilled labor experience a more pronounced reduction in their ability to smooth cash flows because their labor is more costly to adjust. Therefore, investors required return for their investment increases with a firm's reliance on skilled labor. In particular, the model suggests that the compensation for volatility risk and its contribution to risk compensation increases with a firm's reliance on skilled labor.

To test the model implications, I first present empirical evidence supporting the model's assumption of a positive relationship between a worker's skill and the cost of replacing the worker. To this end, I use a unique employee-employer matched data set which contains detailed information on several costs the firm incurred filling the most recent vacant position.[2] Motivated by this evidence, I construct an empirical measure of a firm's reliance on skilled labor as proxy for labor adjustment costs using the Bureau of Labor Statics (BLS) estimates of occupational employment along with the U.S. Department of Labor's classification of occupations based on skill level for 1988 to 2010.

Based on panel regressions, I find that firms which have a large concentration of skilled labor have higher expected returns on equity relative to those in which a larger share of labor is unskilled. This conclusion is robust to whether I include controls for known characteristics that explain the cross-section of expected returns, such as the book-to-market equity ratio, market equity, and past performance, as well as predictors of expected returns which might be correlated with a firm's reliance on skilled labor, such us R&D intensity, profitability, operating costs, investment rate, sensitivity of sales to macroeconomic growth, leverage, and labor intensity.

I also test if aggregate volatility has a positive impact on the risk premium implied by the reliance on skilled labor, as predicted by the model. As in Bloom (2009), I consider implied volatility computed from the old Volatility Index (VIX) and realized volatility computed using daily S&P 500 returns as proxies for aggregate volatility. I find strong empirical evidence suggesting that the risk compensation for a firm's reliance on skilled labor increases with macroeconomic volatility. In terms of economic significance, I find that a one standard deviation increase in a firm's reliance on skilled labor is associated with an increase in annual expected equity returns of about 2.7% in times when aggregate volatility is high. In contrast,

---

[2]Parsons (1986) and more recently Hamermesh and Pfann (1996) survey evidence concluding that these quasi-fixed costs are substantial. They amount to as much as one year of payroll cost for the average worker and seem to increase rapidly with the skill of the worker.

the premium is about 1.0% when volatility is at its historical average.

On top of that, I explore the exposure to aggregate volatility of portfolios sorted on the reliance on skilled labor. First, I find that the risk premium for the reliance on skilled labor, which is the spread in equity returns between the top and bottom quintiles of portfolios sorted on the reliance on skilled labor, is high in times when the variance risk premium is high.[3] Then, I explore if the exposure to fluctuations in aggregate volatility explains the cross-section of expected returns of double-sorted portfolios on the reliance of skilled labor and market equity. The cross-sectional regression results show that the variance risk premium has a negative and statistically significant market price of risk. The single-factor model captures 40.8% of the cross-sectional variation in returns.

Finally, I explore if the risk premium for reliance on skilled labor contains information about systemic risk which is not contained in existing risk factors. To this end, I first show that the risk premium for the reliance on skilled labor is not spanned by the market excess return, the size, the book-to-market and the momentum risk factors. Then, I show that the risk premium for the reliance on skilled labor is able to explain the cross-sectional variation in average equity returns on industry portfolios. When the basic CAPM is augmented with the risk premium for a firm's reliance on skilled labor the adjusted R^2 is 36.6%, and its market price of risk is positive and statistically different from zero. In contrast, the basic CAPM has an adjusted R^2 of 0.1%, while the Fama-French three factor model has an R^2 of only 22.1%.

The ideas in this paper build on and contribute to several strands of the literature. First, the literature exploring the implications for asset returns of time-varying aggregate volatility. Bansal and Yaron (2004) long-run risks model suggests that compensation for fluctuations in aggregate volatility carry a separate and positive risk premium. More recently, Bansal, Kiku, Shaliastovich, and Yaron (2012) present empirical evidence that all equity portfolios have positive compensation for volatility risks. Moreover, volatility risks account for one-half of risk premia in financial markets, and are important in explaining the cross-sectional variation in equity returns. Similarly, Campbell, Giglio, Polk, and Turley (2012) and Bali and Zhou (2012) also find that the exposure of equity portfolios to aggregate volatility predicts the cross-sectional variation in expected returns of characteristic-sorted portfolios. Motivated

---

[3]The variance risk premium is the difference between implied volatility and realized volatility. Bollerslev, Tauchen, and Zhou (2009) show that it captures fluctuations in aggregate economic uncertainty and it is independent from growth risk.

by this evidence, this paper provides an economic model and empirical evidence linking the exposure to aggregate volatility to an observed characteristic of a firm, namely, the reliance on skilled workers.

Second, the literature exploring hiring and investment decisions under uncertainty. Abel and Eberly (1994), Dixit and Pindyck (1994), Dixit (1997), and Stokey (2008) show that a firm's factor demands are characterized by areas of inaction in the presence of non-convex adjustment costs. Uncertainty enlarges this area because the option value of the *status quo* increases. Recently, Bloom (2009) and Bloom, Floetotto, Jaimovich, Saporta-Eksten, and Terry (2012) explore this mechanism in an environment of stochastic volatility, and find that fluctuations in aggregate volatility can lead to bust-boom cycles. Departing from this literature, the model presented here explores the impact of time-varying macroeconomic volatility on a firm's labor demand and its cost of capital, and how they relate to each other. Thus, the model sheds some light on the economic mechanism that links asset markets to the labor market.

Finally, the literature that empirically and theoretically explores the interaction between frictions in the labor market and asset prices. Danthine and Donaldson (2002) propose a general equilibrium model with labor-induced operating leverage. Matsa (2010), Chen, Kacperczyk, and Ortiz-Molina (2011), and Schmalz (2011) explore the impact that unionization has on capital structure decisions and the cost of equity. Donangelo (2011) considers labor mobility, and Merz and Yashiv (2007) and Bazdrech, Belo, and Lin (2009) underscore the importance of labor adjustment costs to explain the risk of equity. The model with convex adjustment costs of Belo and Lin (2013), written independently from and simultaneously with this paper, shows that labor demand responsiveness to changes in the discount rate decreases as adjustment costs increase. Using the industry level of labor skill as a proxy for the industry labor adjustment costs, they find that industries with skilled labor have a more negative expected return-hiring rate relation and higher average stock returns than industries with low-skilled labor. The unconditional spread in returns, however, is robust only for small firms. In contrast to this literature, this paper underscores the importance of non-convex costs and the real-option effect of fluctuations in macroeconomic volatility to understand the cross-sectional variation in expected equity returns. Moreover, it uncovers a novel structural explanation for differences in the exposure to macroeconomic volatility.

2 The Model

This section presents a production-based asset pricing model that builds on the models of labor demand with adjustment costs of Bentolila and Bertola (1990), Caballero, Engel, and Haltiwanger (1997), Cooper and Willis (2009) and adds two ingredients. First, I introduce labor heterogeneity. Firms differ in their reliance on skilled labor, and they face linear adjustment costs in labor which are increasing with the skill of the worker. Second, the model has two sources of macroeconomic risk: fluctuations in aggregate productivity and time-varying volatility of productivity growth. The stochastic discount factor to compute the compensation for these risks and asset prices in general comes from the the long-run risks model of Bansal and Yaron (2004). The model simulations suggest that a firm's reliance on skilled labor is positively related to a firm's exposure to fluctuations in aggregate volatility. Consequently, there is a an increasing monotonic relationship between expected equity returns and a firm's reliance on skilled labor.

2.1 Dynamic Problem of the Firm

The economy is populated by competitive firms which produce output goods y using labor as the only input,

$$y_{i,t} = A_t \left(h_{i,t} n_{i,t}^e\right)^\alpha, \tag{1}$$

where A_t is stochastic aggregate productivity, $h_{i,t}$ is the input of hours per worker, $n_{i,t}^e$ represents the stock of workers measured in efficiency units for firm i at time t. As in Kydland (1984), $n_{i,t}^e$ is a weighted average of a firm's stock of high-skilled n^{hs} and low-skilled n^{ls} workers,

$$n_{i,t}^e = \lambda n_{i,t}^{hs} + n_{i,t}^{ls}, \tag{2}$$

where $\lambda > 1$ represent the relative productivity of high-skilled workers.

Adjustments to labor demand give rise to adjustment costs which include recruiting, selection and hiring costs. Adjusting labor also lead to disruptions in production which translates into a loss of output and productivity. Therefore, I assume that a firm adjusting labor of type j must incur in a cost χ^j for every job it creates or destroys,

$$C^j(n_{i,t}^j, n_{i,t-1}^j) = \chi^j \|n_{i,t}^j - n_{i,t-1}^j\| \quad \text{for } j = hs, ls. \tag{3}$$

I allow the cost χ^j to vary with the skill of a worker, and I assume that the cost of labor adjustment is higher for high-skilled workers than for low-skilled workers, $\chi^{hs} > \chi^{ls}$.

Firms are heterogeneous with respect to the mix of high-skilled and low-skilled workers they use in their production process. In particular, each firm uses a fraction ω_i of high-skilled workers. Consequently, firms that rely heavily on high-skilled workers have higher costs of adjusting labor than firms that rely mostly on low-skilled workers.

Firm's dividends consist of output less the total compensation of workers and costs of labor adjustment,

$$d_{i,t} = y_{i,t} - w(h_{i,t})(\lambda n_{i,t}^{hs} + n_{i,t}^{ls}) - \sum_j C^j(n_{i,t}^j, n_{i,t-1}^j), \tag{4}$$

where the total compensation to high-skilled and low-skilled workers is given by $w(h_{i,t})\lambda n_{i,t}^{hs}$ and $w(h_{i,t})n_{i,t}^{ls}$, respectively. As in Caballero and Engel (1993) and Cooper and Willis (2009), the compensation function $w(h)$ is given by

$$w(h) = w_0 + w_1 h^\zeta, \tag{5}$$

where $\zeta - 1$ is the marginal wage elasticity to hours.

Aggregate productivity growth is stochastic and follows an auto-regressive process with stochastic volatility,

$$\Delta a_t = \mu + \rho \Delta a_{t-1} + \sigma_{t-1} \epsilon_t, \tag{6}$$

where $a_t = \ln A_t$, ϵ_{t+1} is an independent identically distributed standard normal process. Volatility of productivity growth is stochastic and follows a persistent Markov chain capturing the idea that firms uncertainty about aggregate growth fluctuates over time.

The firm's recursive problem is to choose total employment and hours to maximize the market value of the firm by solving

$$\nu_i(\mathbf{s}_{i,t}) = \max_{n_{i,t}, h_{i,t}} y_{i,t} - w(h_{i,t})(\lambda n_{i,t}^{hs} + n_{i,t}^{ls}) - \sum_{j=hs,ls} C^j(n_{i,t}^j, n_{i,t-1}^j) + \mathbb{E}_t\left(M_{t,t+1}\nu_i(\mathbf{s}_{i,t+1})\right) \tag{7}$$

subject to $\omega_i = \frac{n_{i,t}^{hs}}{n_{i,t}^{hs}+n_{i,t}^{ls}}$. Total employment is $n_{i,t} = n_{i,t}^{hs} + n_{i,t}^{ls}$, the state of the economy is given by $\mathbf{s}_{i,t} = (n_{i,t-1}, A_t, \Delta a_t, \sigma_t)$, $\nu_i(\mathbf{s}_{i,t})$ is the cum-dividend market value of firm i at time t, and $M_{t,t+1}$ is the stochastic discount factor. Note that when a firm chooses total employment $n_{i,t}$, the firm's given reliance on high-skilled labor ω_i determines the number of skilled and unskilled workers the firm utilizes, namely, $n_{i,t}^{hs} = \omega_i n_{i,t}$ and $n_{i,t}^{ls} = (1-\omega_i)n_{i,t}$.

The return on firm i's equity is defined as

$$R_{i,t+1} = \frac{\nu_i(\mathbf{s}_{i,t+1})}{\nu_i(\mathbf{s}_{i,t}) - d_{i,t}}. \tag{8}$$

From the Bellman equation (7) characterizing the recursive problem of the firm, it follows directly that $R_{i,t+1}$ satisfies the standard asset pricing restriction condition $1 = \mathbb{E}_t\left(M_{t,t+1} R_{i,t+1}\right)$.

2.2 Stochastic Discount Factor

Firms take as given the stochastic discount factor which is derived from the problem of a representative investor with Epstein and Zin (1989) and Weil (1990) type of recursive preferences. As shown in Bansal and Yaron (2004), this preference structure implies the following stochastic discount factor,

$$M_{t,t+1} = \beta^{\frac{1-\gamma}{1-1/\psi}} \left(\frac{C_{t+1}}{C_t}\right)^{-\gamma} \left(\frac{Z_{t+1}+1}{Z_t}\right)^{\frac{1/\psi-\gamma}{1-1/\psi}},$$

where $0 < \beta < 1$ is the subjective discount factor, γ is the coefficient of risk aversion, and ψ is the intertemporal elasticity of substitution (IES), C_t is the representative investor's consumption, and Z_t is the wealth-consumption ratio. This type of preferences allows a distinction between the coefficient of risk aversion γ and the IES ψ, when $\gamma = \frac{1}{\psi}$ the stochastic discount factor collapses to the case in which the representative investor's preferences are CRRA (constant relative risk aversion). Finally, I assume consumption growth is positively related to technology growth,

$$\Delta c_t = \mu(1-\phi) + \phi \Delta a_{t-1} + \sigma_t \nu_t, \tag{9}$$

where ν_t is an independent identically distributed standard normal stochastic process.

Productivity growth Δa_t and stochastic volatility σ_t are the driving forces behind the fluctuations of both aggregate productivity A_t and consumption C_t; consequently, these are the sources of systemic risk. The stochastic discount factor pertinent for the problem at hand corresponds to the case when the investor has a preference for early resolution of uncertainty, or more specifically to the case where the relative risk aversion is greater than the inverse of the IES $\gamma > 1/\psi$. As shown in Bansal and Yaron (2004), under this assumption the investor dislikes negative shocks to expected consumption growth and unexpected increases in aggregate volatility. Therefore, shocks to volatility will carry a separate risk compensation.

2.3 Calibration

The firm's optimal hiring and firing decisions, the firm's return on equity, and firm's the value are all a function of the state variables of the economy, which I obtain using numerical methods for the set of parameters specified in Table 1. The model is calibrated at a monthly frequency, and the numerical solution method is explained in Appendix A.

The first set of parameters corresponds to preferences of the representative household and the consumption dynamics which are very similar to those reported in Bansal, Kiku, and Yaron (2012). The subjective discount factor β equals 0.9989, the risk aversion parameter γ and the intertemporal elasticity of substitution ψ are equal to 10 and 2, respectively. Under this configuration, the agent has a preference for early resolution of uncertainty which implies that representative investor dislikes negative shocks to expected consumption growth and unexpected increases in aggregate volatility.

Labor share α is set equal to 0.67 which is consistent with the U.S. labor income share (King and Rebelo 1999). The coefficients characterizing the compensation function w_1 and w_0 are chosen so that over the balanced growth path hours per week for each employed worker are equal to 40 and the ratio of workers to productivity $n_t/A^{1/(1-\alpha)}$ is equal to 1, respectively. I set ζ equal to 2.88 which is the empirical estimate of Cooper and Willis (2009). The cost χ^{hs} is set to six months of a worker's wage and χ^{hs} is set to a week of a worker's compensation.

The parameters μ and ρ are set to match the growth rate and persistence consumption growth reported in Bansal, Kiku, and Yaron (2012). Aggregate uncertainty σ_t follows a three-state Markov chain. Using the method detailed in Rouwenhorst (1995) the transition matrix parameters are chosen such that the persistence of volatility equals 0.978 and the monthly volatility of aggregate uncertainty equals 0.003, which are consistent with the quarterly estimates presented in Boguth and Kuehn (2009). The unconditional expected value of σ_t is chosen to match consumption growth volatility.

2.4 Qualitative Properties of the Optimal Employment Choice

In the presence of piecewise linear costs of adjusting labor the optimal decision of the firm consists of two aspects: at what points action should be taken, and what the action should be (Dixit 1993, Stokey 2009). In the model, the firm chooses a state-dependent interval $(b^*(\Delta a_t, \sigma_t), B^*(\Delta a_t, \sigma_t))$ such that when the labor-productivity ratio $\tilde{n}_{i,t}$ is inside this interval the firm chooses inaction, that is, the stock of workers remains unchanged $n_t = n_{t-1}$, whereas when the labor-productivity ratio leaves the inaction region the firm chooses to hire or fire workers. Panel (a) of Figure 1 displays the optimal choice of labor-aggregate productivity ratio $\tilde{n}_{i,t}$ along with the optimal inaction region (b^*, B^*). While the labor-productivity ratio $\tilde{n}_{i,t-1}$ remains inside the inaction region the firm chooses inaction. If aggregate productivity increases sufficiently such that the labor-productivity ratio falls below b^*, the firm immediately hires workers so that the labor-productivity ratio is equal to the lower barrier b^*. In contrast, if productivity falls sufficiently such that the labor-productivity ratio increases above B^*, the firm will fire workers such that the labor-productivity ratio achieves the upper barrier point B^*.

Panel (b) of Figure 1 displays the impact of variations in aggregate volatility on the optimal inaction regions. An increase in aggregate volatility σ_t enlarges the range of inaction because the possibility that a firm may find hiring or firing unwarranted increases. In particular, b^* decreases sharply as uncertainty increases but has very little impact on B^*. Consequently, the firm will wait until aggregate economic conditions are sufficiently good to start hiring when volatility is high compared to times when it is low. In this environment in which aggregate volatility fluctuates, the presence of piecewise linear costs implies that inactivity in employment adjustment increases as economic conditions become more uncertain.[4]

---

[4]This result is consistent with the standard comparative static result presented in Stokey (2009) where the optimal thresholds are computed comparing permanent differences in volatility.

2.5 Implications for the Cross-section of Equity Returns

Panel (a) of Figure 2 displays the average equity return on a firm with a share of skilled workers ω in excess of the return on the firm with the lowest ω along different values of ω, $\mathbb{E}(R_\omega - R_{\underline{\omega}})$. The model predicts that expected excess returns increase with a firm's reliance on skilled labor (i.e., as ω increases). What is the contribution of fluctuations in aggregate volatility to differences in expected equity returns? Figure 3 displays expected excess returns for different values of ω, $\mathbb{E}(R_\omega - R_{\underline{\omega}})$. The line with circular markers comes from the baseline model assuming time-varying aggregate volatility while the line with cross markers corresponds to the case in which aggregate volatility is constant. The simulation results suggest that the compensation for volatility risk increases with a firm's reliance on skilled workers. Moreover, compensation for volatility risk is quantitatively more important for firms with a high share of skilled workers, consequently, it explains a larger portion of the risk compensation for firms with a high share of skilled labor than compensation for growth risks. In line with this implication, Panel (b) of Figure 2 shows that in the model a rise in aggregate volatility predicts an increase in the risk compensation for the reliance on skilled workers suggesting that a firm's exposure to fluctuations in aggregate volatility increases with its reliance on skilled labor.

To better understand the link between a firm's reliance on skilled labor and expected excess returns it is helpful to inspect the optimal inaction region for a firm with high share of unskilled workers, high-ω, and one with a low share of skilled workers, low-ω (see Figure 4). An increase in aggregate volatility widens the inaction region slowing a firm's labor demand reaction to changes in economic conditions, and this effect is larger for the high-ω firm since its labor is more costly to adjust. Consequently, the high-ω firm experiences a more pronounced reduction in its ability to smooth cash-flows than a low-ω firm because the high-ω firm is expected to spend more time inside the inaction region. All in all, the model suggests that a firm's reliance on skilled labor is positively related to a firm's exposure to fluctuations in aggregate volatility because their labor is more costly to adjust, therefore, investors' required compensation for their investment will also increase with a firm's reliance on skilled labor.

3 Empirical Evidence

This section empirically tests the implications of the model. I start this section by presenting empirical evidence supporting the model's assumption of a positive relationship between a worker's skill and the cost of replacing the worker. Then, using a firm's reliance on occupations with high levels of skill as a proxy for labor adjustment costs, I find a positive and statistically significant cross-sectional relation between the reliance on skilled labor and equity returns. Consistent with the model, the spread of average returns between firms with high and low share of skilled workers increases with aggregate volatility. These results are robust even after controlling for predictors of average equity returns known in the literature which are unrelated to the costs of adjusting labor, but that are possibly correlated with the concentration of skilled labor in a firm. Furthermore, I present evidence that the reliance on skilled labor premium is not spanned by known risk factors and contains additional information about aggregate volatility risk.

3.1 Worker's Skill and Labor Adjustment Costs

There are few studies that quantify the extent of labor adjustment costs, and much less the relationship between a worker's skill level and such costs because most labor adjustment costs are implicit and are not measured or reported on a firm's accounting records (Hamermesh and Pfann 1996).[5] Some studies concerning single firms or industries have concluded that the costs of adjusting labor are large and they amount to as much as one year of payroll cost for the average worker, and these costs increase very rapidly with the skill of the worker.[6]

This section presents empirical evidence supporting a positive relationship between a worker's skill and the costs of replacing the worker. In the analysis I use the firm-level data from the 1980 Employer Opportunity Pilot Project (EOPP), a unique employee-employer matched data set, which contains information on about 5,200 firms from ten different states in the U.S. and different industries. The EOPP data set contains detailed information on costs the firm incurred filling the most recent vacant position, namely, the time spent

---

[5] For example, when new employees join a work crew, senior employees spend time training them, and disruptions in production may arise leading to a loss in productivity and output.

[6] See, for example, Oi (1962), Mincer (1962), Merchants and Manufacturers Association (1980) survey, Pfann and Verspagen (1989), Button (1990), and Cascio (1991). Similarly, Dolfin (2006) finds that higher costs are associated with lower turnover rates, and turnover rates are higher for unskilled workers.

recruiting for the position, the number of applicants interviewed, the amount of time employees and supervisory staff spent training the new hire the first month of employment, and the new hire's level of productivity during the second week of employment. It also contains information on the recent hire's education, relevant job experience, and gender. The employer also provides information about maximum hourly wage for the position filled by the last new hire, as well as the productivity level of the last employee in that position.[7]

Table 2 presents summary statistics of the relevant variables as well as means conditional on the education of the new employee. From the sample of firms, 69% reported a newly hired. On average, these firms spent 18 days recruiting, interviewed about five candidates, during the employee's first month of tenure superiors and employees spent 32.8 hours away from normal work routines orienting and training recent hire, and during the second week of employment the employee was on average 15.6% less productive than the person she replaced on that occupation. The results also show that the unconditional mean of each of these labor adjustment costs is higher for new employees with a high-school diploma or more, relative to new hires with no high-school

To explore how these costs vary with the skill of the new hire using a multivariate analysis, I estimate the following model,

$$cost_i = \alpha + \beta \ skill_i + \mathbf{x}'_i \delta + u_i, \qquad (10)$$

where $cost_i$ is a component of labor adjustment costs for position i, and $skill$ corresponds to a measure of skill, and u_i is the error term. I use two alternative measures of skill, the education of the newly hired and the top hourly wage for that position. It is reasonable to assume that the education of the newly hired and the maximum hourly wage for the position are both positively related to the level of skill the employer needs to fill the vacant position. The vector $\mathbf{x}$ of control variables contains age, gender and relevant experience of the recent new hire, as well as the size of the firm computed as the number of full-time and part-time employees and dummy variables to control for fixed industry characteristics at the 3-digit SIC level.

First, I explore the relationship between the education of the newly hired and labor adjustment costs. Table 3 presents the estimated coefficients from equation (10) where

---

[7]The information is about the last position filled between January 1978 and October 1979. The Data Appendix contains the specific questions for gathering labor adjustment costs.

each column considers as a dependent variable one of the following costs of filling a vacant position: the number of days an employer spent filling the position, the number of applicants interviewed for the position, the hours spent by employees and supervisors training the last new hire, and the last new hire productivity gap defined as the productivity of the last employee in the position relative to the productivity of the new employee during the second week of employment. Education is a dummy variable which is equal to 1 if the new employee has a high-school diploma or more years of education. The estimated coefficient on education of the recent new hire is positive and statistically different from zero across all components of labor adjustment costs. For example, if the new hire has a high-school diploma or more, the expected number of days recruiting increases by about 6, employers expect to interview two more candidates, employees provide 4.6 more hours of training, and the new hire's productivity gap is about 3.1% higher. Similar evidence arises when I use the (log) max wage per hour for that position as proxy of the new hire's skill (see Table 4). The estimated coefficients imply that the time recruiting increases by 15 days when the position's top wage doubles. Similarly, the number of people interviewed increases by two, the hours of training go up by 18, and the productivity gap is 5.3 percentage points higher.

All in all, the empirical evidence presented in Tables 3 and 4 support the model's assumption that the cost of replacing a worker increases with the skill of the worker. Moreover, it also suggests that it is reasonable to use increasing skill levels as a proxy for increasing adjustment costs. Hence, given that most labor adjustment costs are not reported by firms, in the empirical exercises I use a firm's reliance on skilled labor as a proxy for labor adjustment costs as in Oi (1962) and Rosen (1968).

I compute a firm's reliance on skilled labor as a skill-weighted average of the number of workers using information on occupational employment, namely,

$$\text{LSKILL}_j = \sum_{i=1}^{O} \lambda_i \frac{L_{ij}}{L_j}, \qquad (11)$$

where L_{ij} is the number of employees in industry j at occupation i, L_j is the total number of employees in industry j, and λ_i is the skill-level of occupation i. To compute this measure I use the Occupational Employment Statistics (OES) estimates of occupational employment at the 3-digit SIC classification along with the U.S. Department of Labor's O*NET program classification of occupations based on skill. This program classifies occupations into five "job zones," ranging from job zone 1, $\lambda_i = 1$, which includes occupations that need little or no skills (e.g., counter and rental clerks, construction laborers, and waiters/waitresses) to job zone 5, $\lambda_i = 5$, which consists of occupations that need extensive skill levels (e.g., lawyers, aerospace engineers, surgeons, treasurers, and controllers).[8] Consequently, low values of LSKILL imply that the industry's majority of occupations need little or no skill to perform their job, while high values of LSKILL imply that a large share of the industry's occupations are filled with employees who need extensive skill levels to adequately perform their job. Appendix B contains a more detailed description of the data sources.

Table 5 presents summary statistics of the cross-sectional and time-series variation in the reliance on skilled labor for selected industries with the highest and lowest values of LSKILL for the period of 1988-2010. The reliance on skilled labor LSKILL shows important cross-sectional variation across industries. The industries with the highest values of LSKILL have a value around 3.5 (e.g., engineering and architectural services, legal services) while the bottom three industries' LSKILL value is below 1.5 (e.g., maintenance services to buildings, automobile parking, eating and drinking places). On the other hand, the reliance on skilled labor index does not show much time-series variation, which suggests that most of the variation in the workers' skill index comes from cross-sectional differences. The list of industries in Table 5 also suggests that defining a firm's industry membership by its 3-digit SIC groups together firms that are in similar lines of business as argued in the work of Hou and Robinson (2006). The sample contains information for 312 industries.

3.2 Data Sources for Financial and Macroeconomic Variables

For the empirical exercises, I use monthly stock returns from the Center for Research in Security Prices (CRSP), and accounting information from the CRSP/COMPUSAT Merged Annual Industrial Files. The sample of firms includes all NYSE-, AMEX-, and NASDAQ-listed securities which are identified by CRSP as ordinary common shares (with share codes 10 and 11) for the period between January 1987 and June 2011. Following Fama and French (2008), the sample excludes banks and financial firms (Standard Industrial Classification codes between 6000 and 6999), and firms with negative book equity in $t-1$.

I use a firm's industry membership as defined by the 3-digit SIC code to match the

---

[8] Alternatively, the level of skill of an occupation λ can also be approximated by the hourly wage of an occupation. In fact, the job zones defined by the Department of Labor are highly correlated with the hourly wage on each occupation. However, I use the index computed using the job zones because the OES program started collecting information on wages only after 1999.

firm with its corresponding reliance on skilled labor (LSKILL). The empirical exercises also use information about a firm's (log) book-to-market equity (lnBM), (log) market equity (lnME), R&D intensity (R&D) measured as R&D expenditures as a share of the firm's market equity, operating leverage (OL) measured as the ratio of operating costs to total assets value, profitability (E/A+) measured as positive earnings before interest divided by total assets, assets growth (ASSETG) defined as the annual growth in asset value, sales beta (SALESB) measured as the slope coefficient from a regression of a firm's annual growth in sales on annual GDP growth using quarterly data, labor intensity (LABORINT) defined as the ratio of number of employees to total assets value, and total leverage (LEV) measured as the ratio of book liabilities (total assets minus book equity) to total market value of firm (market equity plus total assets minus book equity).

I also use aggregate macroeconomic variables for the U.S.. I use the 3-month Treasury-bill rate from the Federal Reserve Bank at St. Louis data base FRED to compute the return on equity in excess of the risk free rate. I compute the log of the earnings price ratio (lnE/P) and the default corporate spread (DFSP) defined as the difference between BAA and AA-rated corporate bond yields using data from Welch and Goyal (2008). I compute inflation using the Consumer Price Index from the Bureau of Labor Statistics. I consider two proxies of aggregate volatility: implied volatility computed using the VXO index based on S&P 100 index options, and realized volatility computed as the monthly standard deviation of the daily S&P 500 index. As shown in Bloom (2009) and Bloom, Floetotto, Jaimovich, Saporta-Eksten, and Terry (2012), these two measures of aggregate stock market volatility are strongly correlated with other measures of productivity and demand uncertainty such as the cross-sectional standard deviation of firms' pre-tax profit growth, the standard deviation of Total Factor Productivity growth within the manufacturing sector, and the dispersion over GDP growth predictions of professional forecasters. Finally, I obtain the variance risk premium (VRP) from Zhou (2010) which is computed as the difference between implied volatility and realized volatility as proposed in Bollerslev, Tauchen, and Zhou (2009).

I match CRSP monthly stock return data from July of year t to June of $t+1$ with accounting information from the fiscal year ending in year $t-1$ and with the reliance on skilled labor LSKILL computed in May of year t. The sample contains 756,355 observations for 10,890 firms across 312 industries for the period of 1988 to 2010. Table 6 presents the summary statistics of the variables used in the empirical exercises.

3.3 Reliance on Skilled Labor and Expected Equity Returns

I start by exploring the predictive power of the reliance on skill labor (LSKILL) on the cross-section of expected returns. Table 7 presents the estimated coefficients from a regression of firm-level monthly stock returns on LSKILL controlling for known predictors of average returns, namely,

$$r_{ij,t+1} = \alpha + \beta_1 \text{LSKILL}_{j,t} + \mathbf{x}'_{ij,t}\gamma + u_{ij,t+1}, \qquad (12)$$

where r_{ij} is the monthly stock return of firm i from industry j in excess of the risk-free rate, $\text{LSKILL}_{j,t}$ is the reliance on skilled labor at industry j, and $\mathbf{x}_{ij,t}$ is a vector which includes firm's characteristics, and dummy variables to control for major SIC-division and year fixed-effects to control for differences in the cost of equity across industries and across time. The table also reports standard errors that are corrected for cross-sectional correlation at the 3-digit SIC industry level.

In column (1) of Table 7, as a first exercise, I control for the following firm's characteristics: (log) book-to-market equity ratio (lnBM), (log) market equity (lnME), past performance (PASTRET), and R&D intensity (R&D). The coefficient on LSKILL is positive and statistically significant at the 1% level. This result suggests that firms which have a high concentration of skilled labor have higher expected returns than those in which a larger share of their employees require little or no skills. To explore if LSKILL is not capturing the impact of omitted predictors of average equity returns already known in the literature which are unrelated to the costs of adjusting labor in columns (2) through (7), I include sequentially the following firm's characteristics: operating leverage (OL), profitability (E/A+), assets growth (ASSETG), cyclicality of revenues (SALESB), labor intensity (LABINT), and leverage (LEV).[9] After controlling for these variables, the estimated coefficient on LSKILL remains positive and statistically different from zero. Moreover, the coefficients on the additional control variables have the expected signs and are statistically significant which suggests that the reliance on skilled labor LSKILL has additional information about the risk of equity not captured by these known predictors of expected returns. In terms of magnitude, the

---

[9] Chan, Lakonishok, and Sougiannis (2001), Li (2011) and Lin (2012) find a positive relation between R&D intensity and expected stock returns. Novy-Marx (2011) shows that firms with higher levels of operating leverage have higher average equity returns. Similarly, Haugen and Baker (1996) and Cohen, Gompers, and Vuolteenaho (2002) find that firms with higher levels of profitability have higher expected returns, and Fairfield, Whisenant, and Yohn (2003), Titman, Wei, and Xie (2004), and Bazdrech, Belo, and Lin (2009) find that firms that invest more have lower expected returns. Pratt (2011) finds that firms that are labor intensive will have lower leverage because they face higher costs of distress.

coefficient on LSKILL across all specifications suggests that a one standard deviation increase in the reliance of skilled labor leads to an increase in annual expected equity returns of about 1.6%.[10]

A similar conclusion emerges when I explore the spread in realized average returns of five portfolios sorted on LSKILL. In the spirit of Fama and French (1993), in June of each year I sort firms according to their reliance on skilled labor into five portfolios, and I compute monthly equally- and value-weighted returns on these portfolios from July through June of the following year. Table 8 presents monthly excess returns for July of 1988 to the end of June of 2011 on these five portfolios along with the test for monotonicity proposed in Wolak (1989). The average excess returns are increasing in the reliance on skilled labor LSKILL, and the difference in returns between the top and bottom quintiles is positive for both the equally-weighted and value-weighted portfolios, and it is statistically significant for the equally-weighted portfolio. In particular, the spread is 0.426% (5.2% in annual terms) and 0.246% (3.0% in annual terms) for the equally-weighted and value-weighted portfolios, respectively. The Wolak (1989) test cannot reject the null of an increasing relation between excess returns and the reliance on skilled labor. These set of tests are consistent with the presence of a monotonically increasing relationship between excess returns and the reliance on skilled labor for both equally-weighted and value-weighted portfolios.

Consistent with the theoretical model, the empirical evidence supports a positive relationship between a firm's reliance on skilled labor and expected equity returns. However, the model's most important implication is that expected equity returns should rise when aggregate volatility is high, and the increase should be more pronounced for firms that rely more heavily on skilled labor. To quantify the impact of aggregate volatility on the premium implied by the reliance on skilled labor, I estimate equation (12) and I allow the coefficient on LSKILL to vary with aggregate volatility, that is,

$$r_{ij,t+1} = \alpha + (\beta_1 + \beta_2 \sigma_t) \times \text{LSKILL}_{j,t} + \mathbf{x}'_{ij,t}\gamma + \beta_3 \sigma_t + u_{ij,t+1}, \tag{13}$$

where σ is a measure of aggregate volatility, r_{ij} is the monthly stock return of firm i from

---

[10] In unreported regressions, I check that the results are not driven by small market capitalization firms, or by extreme values observed on individual stocks. To asses if the predictive power of LSKILL is not driven by small market capitalization firms I compute weighted estimates in which firms are weighted according to their market capitalization, and to minimize the impact of extreme returns I construct industry portfolios defining a firm's industry membership by its three-digit SIC code. In both exercises the coefficient on LSKILL is also positive and statistically significant.

industry j in excess of the risk-free rate, LSKILL$_{j,t}$ is the reliance on skilled labor at industry j, and $\mathbf{x}_{ij,t}$ is a vector which includes the set of firm's characteristics included in the initial specification (12) as well as industry fixed-effects. As in the previous exercise, I first estimate the model controlling for (log) book-to-market equity ratio (lnBM), (log) market equity (lnME), past performance (PASTRET), and R&D intensity (R&D). Then, I present results including all additional firm's characteristics.

Table 9 presents the estimated coefficients of equation (13) where odd-numbered columns use implied volatility IVOL as a proxy for aggregate volatility and even-numbered columns use realized volatility RVOL as a proxy. To ease interpretation, I standardize the two measures of aggregate volatility. As suggested by the theoretical model, the coefficient on the interaction between aggregate volatility and the reliance on skilled labor is positive and statistically different from zero for both proxies of aggregate volatility and in all specifications. The estimated coefficients imply that the LSKILL premium is higher in times of high aggregate volatility than in times of low aggregate volatility. In terms of economic significance, when IVOL is one standard deviation above its historical mean, a one standard deviation increase in LSKILL results in an annual premium of about 2.7%, while in times where IVOL is at its average level the premium is about 1.0%. Similarly, when RVOL is one standard deviation above its historical mean, the premium arising from a one standard deviation increase in LSKILL is about 1.9%, more than twice than in normal times when it is about 0.9%. Controlling for additional firm characteristics does not have any impact on the statistical or economic significance of the LSKILL premium.

The results from Tables 7 through 9 show that the empirical evidence is consistent with the predictions of the model presented in Section 2. When economic conditions are more uncertain (i.e., aggregate volatility is high) investors increase the required rate of return for their investment, and the increase in the cost of equity will be more pronounced for firms that rely more heavily on skilled labor. The model suggests that this is explained by heterogeneity i labor adjustment costs. Therefore, it is unlikely that the results are driven by a firm characteristic unrelated to the cost of adjusting labor.

3.4 Reliance on Skilled Labor and Variance Risk-Premium

The panel regression analysis presented thus far points towards a statistically and economically significant positive relationship between expected returns on equity and the reliance on skilled labor, which increases in times of high aggregate volatility. In this section, I explore the time-series variation of the LSKILL premium, which I compute as the spread in returns between the top and bottom quintiles of portfolios sorted on the reliance on skilled labor LSKILL, and the exposure to aggregate volatility of portfolios sorted on LSKILL.

First, I test if the time-series variation in the reliance on skill labor premium is driven by fluctuations in macroeconomic uncertainty and not by other factors linked to the business cycle. To control for other variables linked to the business cycle, I estimate the following time-series model,

$$rp_{t+1} = \alpha + \beta_1 \text{IVOL}_t + \mathbf{x}'_t \beta + u_{t+1}, \tag{14}$$

where rp_{t+1} is the LSKILL premium, IVOL is standardized implied volatility, and the vector $\mathbf{x}_t$ includes the log earnings-price ratio (lnE/P), the default spread (DFSP), and inflation (INF). The first two columns of Table 10 present the estimated coefficients for equally- and value-weighted measures of the LSKILL premium. Consistent with the panel regressions, the results show that the coefficient on IVOL is positive and statistically significant even after controlling for variables linked to the business cycle.

To further explore if the premium for LSKILL is mainly driven by compensation for volatility risk, I estimate model (14) and replace IVOL by the difference between the implied and expected volatility, that is, the variance risk premium VRP. Bollerslev, Tauchen, and Zhou (2009) and Zhou (2010) show that this measure has the advantage that it is a good proxy for aggregate economic uncertainty and it is independent from growth risk. The last two columns of Table 10 report the estimated coefficients of these regressions for equally- and value-weighted measures of the LSKILL premium. Consistent with the implications of the theoretical model, the LSKILL premium is high in times when the aggregate variance risk premium is high.

As a final exercise, I explore if the exposure to fluctuations in aggregate volatility explains the cross-section of expected equity returns on portfolios sorted on the reliance on skilled labor using the variance risk premium of Bollerslev, Tauchen, and Zhou (2009) as a risk factor. For this purpose, I use the two-stage cross-sectional regression method of Fama and MacBeth (1973), and consider 25 portfolios sorted on size and LSKILL and 5 LSKILL sorted portfolios. First, I estimate the VRP beta as the slope coefficient of a time-series regression of excess returns on each portfolio and the VRP. In the second stage, I run a cross-sectional regression of the average excess equity returns on the 30 portfolios on a constant and the

VRP beta.

The 25 portfolios sorted on size and LSKILL are based on the intersection of 5 portfolios formed on market equity (size) and 5 portfolios formed on LSKILL, which are constructed at the end of each June. Similar to the simple LSKILL portfolio sorts, the spread in average equity returns between the the top and bottom portfolios sorted on LSKILL is positive for all except one of the size quintiles. Also, the 30 portfolios show a positive relationship between average equity returns and LSKILL.

Figure 5 displays a scatter plot of the observed average returns and average returns implied by the cross-sectional model along with the estimated coefficients of the cross-sectional regression. The table also reports t-statistics using the Fama-MacBeth procedure, t-statistics corrected for sampling error in the betas as suggested in Jagannathan and Wang (1998), and the GLS–R^2 as suggested in Lewellen, Nagel, and Shanken (2010). The model has an R^2 of 40.8%, and the coefficient on the variance risk premium beta is negative and statistically different from zero. This implies that portfolios that have a bad performance in times when the aggregate volatility is high (i.e., VRP beta is negative) will have a positive variance risk compensation, and higher expected equity returns. Consistent with the model, firm's that rely more heavily on skilled labor are also more exposed to fluctuations in aggregate volatility and have higher average returns.

3.5 Reliance on Skilled Labor Premium as a Risk Factor

The results presented in the previous section suggest that the reliance on skilled labor risk premium must contain information about systemic risk, in particular, information about aggregate volatility risk. To corroborate this assertion, I first explore the relationship of the LSKILL risk premium and existing risk factors. Then, I explore whether the LSKILL premium is able to explain the cross-sectional variation in average excess equity returns on 47 industry portfolios from Kenneth French's data library.

First, I run a regression of the LSKILL risk premium, computed as the spread in returns between the top and bottom quintiles of portfolios sorted on LSKILL, on the market excess return (MKT), the size risk factor (SMB), the book to market risk factor (HML), and the momentum factor (UMD) to explore if the LSKILL risk premium remains significant after taking into account these well known risk factors. The estimated coefficients and Newey-

West standard errors are reported in Table 11. The results show that the intercept remains positive and statistically significant suggesting that the reliance on skilled labor risk premium contains independent information about the cross-section of average equity returns.

The reliance on skilled labor premium is not spanned by known risk factors, but it is still a question whether it contains information about systemic risk. Therefore, I explore whether the LSKILL risk premium is able to explain the cross-sectional variation in average excess equity returns on 47 industry portfolios. Fama and French (1997) show that industry portfolios are particularly challenging to explain for both the CAPM and their three-factor model. Following the standard cross-sectional regression techniques, I estimate the following asset pricing model,

$$\mathbb{E}(r_i) = \lambda_0 + \lambda_{lskill}\beta_{lskill,i} + \lambda_{mkt}\beta_{mkt,i}, \tag{15}$$

where $\beta_{lskill,i}$ is the univariate beta of the industry portfolio i with respect to the LSKILL risk premium, and $\beta_{mkt,i}$ is the univariate market beta. $\beta_{lskill,i}$ is estimated as the OLS slope coefficient of a regression of the portfolio's excess return on a constant and the LSKILL risk premium. Similarly, $\beta_{mkt,i}$ is the slope coefficient of an OLS regression of the excess return on portfolio i on a constant and the market excess return.

Table 12 presents the estimated coefficients along with Fama and MacBeth (1973) and Jagannathan and Wang (1998) t-statistics from the cross-sectional regression (15). The model has an R^2 of 36.6% and a GLS R^2 of 35.5%, while the market price of risk on the LSKILL premium is positive and statistically different from zero as expected. To assess the performance of this model, Table 12 also presents the cross-sectional regression results from the basic CAPM model and the three-factor (Fama and French 1993) model. The results show that the CAPM fails in explaining the cross-sectional variation in expected industry excess returns. The estimated price of risk is negative and not statistically significant and the R^2 is 0.1%. The Fama-French three-factor model also underperforms the baseline model. The OLS and GLS R^2s are 22.1% and 20.6%, respectively, nearly half the size of the R^2 of the model with LSKILL premium as a risk factor. Moreover, none of the three factors are statistically different from zero.

4 Conclusion

This paper explores and uncovers a novel structural explanation for differences in the exposure to aggregate volatility, namely, a firm's reliance on skilled labor. I propose a production-based asset pricing model in which firms make decisions of firing and hiring in face of time-varying macroeconomic volatility and non-convex labor adjustment costs which increase with the skill of a worker. The model suggests that firms' exposure to aggregate volatility is closely related to its reliance on skilled labor through the following economic mechanism. An increase in aggregate uncertainty slows a firm's labor demand reaction to changes in economic conditions, reducing its ability to smooth cash flows. This phenomenon is more pronounced at firms with a high share of skilled workers because their labor is more costly to adjust. Consequently, these firms are more exposed to fluctuations in aggregate uncertainty and investors command a higher return for investing in these type of firms.

Consistent with the implications of the model, I present empirical evidence showing that investors demand higher expected returns for holding stocks of firms with a high reliance on skilled labor relative to stocks of firms with a low reliance on skilled labor. Moreover, the risk premium for a firm's reliance on skilled labor increases with aggregate volatility. These conclusions are robust to whether I include controls for known characteristics that explain the cross-section of expected returns, and to alternative empirical strategies. I also find that the premium for the reliance on skilled labor contains information about systemic risk, in particular, information about aggregate volatility risk.

Appendix

A   Numerical Solution Algorithm

Solving the Stochastic Discount Factor

To solve for the stochastic discount factor note that the return on wealth satisfies the standard asset pricing restriction condition,

$$1 = \mathbb{E}_t \left(M_{t,t+1} R_{c,t+1} \right), \tag{16}$$

which can be written as,

$$1 = \mathbb{E}_t \left(\beta^{\frac{1-\gamma}{1-1/\psi}} \left(\frac{C_{t+1}}{C_t} \right)^{1-\gamma} \left(\frac{Z_{t+1}}{Z_t - 1} \right)^{\frac{1-\gamma}{1-1/\psi}} \right). \tag{17}$$

The state variables, Δa_t and σ_t, in the model follow a Markov chain; therefore the wealth-consumption ratio is a time-invariant function of the state variables $Z_t = Z(\Delta a_t, \sigma_t)$. Replacing consumption growth using equation (9) and making explicit the dependence of the wealth consumption ratio on the state variables we have that $Z(\Delta a_t, \sigma_t)$ must solve the following system of equations,

$$1 = \mathbb{E}_{\Delta a_t, \sigma_t} \left(\beta^{\frac{1-\gamma}{1-1/\psi}} \exp\left((1-\gamma)(\mu + \phi(\Delta a_t - \mu) + \sigma_t \eta_{t+1})\right) \left(\frac{Z(\Delta a_{t+1}, \sigma_{t+1})}{Z(\Delta a_t, \sigma_t) - 1} \right)^{\frac{1-\gamma}{1-1/\psi}} \right). \tag{18}$$

Solving the Dynamic Problem of the Firm

Equation (7) presents the recursive problem of the firm,

$$\nu(\mathbf{s}_t) = \max_{n_t, h_t} A_t (n_t^e h_t)^\alpha - w(h_t, n_t^e) - \sum_{j=hs,ls} C^j(n_t^j, n_{t-1}^j) + \mathbb{E}_t \left(M_{t,t+1} \nu(\mathbf{s}_{t+1}) \right) \tag{19}$$

where I suppressed any firm specific subscript to save notation.

To obtain the stationary representation of the firm's problem, let

$$\tilde{n}_t = \frac{n_t}{A_t^{1/(1-\alpha)}}$$

and let
$$\frac{C^j(n_t^j, n_{t-1}^j)}{A_t^{1/(1-\alpha)}} = C^j\left(\tilde{n}_t^j, \left(\frac{A_t}{A_{t-1}}\right)^{-1/(1-\alpha)} \tilde{n}_{t-1}^j\right) \qquad (20)$$

then, the stationary representation of the recursive problem is given by,

$$\tilde{\nu}(n_{t-1}, \Delta a_t, \sigma_t) = \max_{\tilde{n}_t} \left(((\lambda\omega + 1 - \omega)n_t h_t^*)^\alpha - (w_0 + w_1 h_t^{*\phi})(\theta\omega + 1 - \omega)n_t \right.$$
$$- C^1\left(\omega n_t, \left(\frac{A_t}{A_{t-1}}\right)^{-1/(1-\alpha)} \omega n_{t-1}\right) - C^2\left((1-\omega)n_t, \left(\frac{A_t}{A_{t-1}}\right)^{-1/(1-\alpha)} (1-\omega)n_{t-1}\right)$$
$$\left. + \mathbb{E}_t\left(M_{t,t+1}\left(\frac{A_{t+1}}{A_t}\right)^{1/(1-\alpha)} \tilde{\nu}(n_t, \Delta a_{t+1}, \sigma_{t+1})\right) \right)$$

where the optimal hours satisfy,

$$h_t^* = \left(\frac{\alpha A_t((\lambda\omega + 1 - \omega)n_t)^{\alpha-1}}{w_1 \zeta}\right)^{\frac{1}{\zeta-\alpha}} \qquad (21)$$

and $\tilde{\nu}(n_{t-1}, \Delta a_t, \sigma_t)$ is equal to $\frac{\nu(n_{t-1}, A_t, \Delta a_t, \sigma_t)}{A_t^{1/(1-\alpha)}}$.

I solve the stationary representation of the model using value function iteration. To accelerate convergence, I use the multi-grid algorithm of Chow and Tsitsiklis (1991) and policy function iteration as described in Rust (1996). The final number of grids for optimal employment-productivity ratio $\tilde{n}_t$ is 800, and I use nine states to approximate the dynamics of Δa_t.

B Data

Employment Opportunities Pilot Projects (EOPP) 1980

The analysis in Section 3.1 uses data from the Employment Opportunities Pilot Projects (EOPP) employer survey conducted during 1980 and funded by the Department of Labor's Employment and Training Administration. The survey was designed to test the effects of an intensive job search program on employers, individuals and families, and local and national economies. The EOPP employer survey was conducted with a total of about 5,918 employers, and includes all non-agricultural for-profit employers that have unemployment insurance accounts across nine states of the U.S.. The variables measuring costs related to labor adjustment are constructed from the following questions from the questionnaire to employers:

- Time spent recruiting: Approximately how long was it between the time the employer started to recruit for the job and the last employee started work?

- Number of persons interviewed for position: How many applicants, including the last employee, were interviewed for the position?

- Hours training corresponds to hours training of employees as well as supervisory staff:
    - In the first month of the last employee's employment, approximately how many hours did employees other than personnel and supervisory staff, spend away from their normal work routines orienting and training (him/her)?
    - In the first month of the last employee's employment, approximately how many hours did personnel and supervisory staff, spend away from their normal work routines orienting and training (him/her)?

- Productivity loss is the difference between the productivity of the worker previously in the position and the newly hired:
    - If you consider the productivity of an average experienced worker in this job to be 50 on a scale from 1 to 100, what rating would you give the last employee for (his/her) productivity at the time of separation?
    - If you consider the productivity of an average experienced worker in this job to be 50 on a scale from 1 to 100, what rating would you give the last employee for (his/her) productivity during the second week of employment?

Occupational Employment and Skill

In section 3.1, I compute an industry's reliance on skilled labor combining data from the Bureau of Labor Statistics Occupational Employment Statistics (OES) program and the

Occupational Information Network (O*NET). The OES program produces employment and wage estimates for 840 detailed occupations. Since 1999, the OES program uses the Standard Occupational Classification (SOC) system to classify workers and jobs into occupations, and before 1999 the OES program used the Occupational Employment Statistics (OES) system. To ensure a consistent classification of occupations over my sample period, 1988–2011, I use the crosswalk files provided by the National Crosswalk Service Center. OES data is available from 1988 to now except for the year 1996, which I proxy using information from 1995. The OES provides national industry-specific employment data, however, from 1988 through 1995 not all industries were surveyed each year. Therefore, employment is computed as a rolling three-year average over this period.

To quantify the level of skill of each occupation, I use the Department of Labor's Employment and Training Administration's O*NET program classification of occupations based on how much education, related work experience and how much on-the-job training an employee needs to perform the work at a competent level. Specifically, the O*NET program classifies occupations into five groups or Job Zones. Job Zone 1 includes occupations that do not usually require a high school diploma, little or no previous work-related experience, skill or knowledge is needed, and people in these occupations need from few days to few months of training. While a Job Zone 5 includes occupations which require education at the graduate level (e.g., master's degree, Ph.D., M.D. or J.D.), and require extensive skill, knowledge and experience. The O*NET program classifies occupations according to the SOC and has information on 974 occupations.

References

Abel, Andrew B., and Janice C. T3 Eberly, 1994, A Unified Model of Investment Under Uncertainty, *The American Economic Review* 84, 1369–1384.

Bali, T, and H Zhou, 2012, Risk, uncertainty, and expected returns, Sixth Singapore International Conference on Finance 2012 Paper.

Bansal, R., V. Khatchatrian, and A. Yaron, 2005, Interpretable asset markets?, *European Economic Review* 49, 531–560.

Bansal, R, D Kiku, I Shaliastovich, and A Yaron, 2012, Volatility, the Macroeconomy and Asset Prices, Forthcoming Journal of Finance.

Bansal, Ravi, Dana Kiku, and Amir Yaron, 2012, An Empirical Evaluation of the Long-Run Risks Model for Asset Prices, *Critical Finance Review* 1, 183–221.

Bansal, Ravi, and Amir Yaron, 2004, Risks for the long run: A potential resolution of asset pricing puzzles, *The Journal of Finance* 59, 1481–1509.

Bazdrech, Santiago, Frederico Belo, and Xiaoji Lin, 2009, Labor Hiring, Investment and Stock Return Predictability in the Cross Section, .

Bekaert, Geert, Eric Engstrom, and Yuhang Xing, 2009, Risk, uncertainty, and asset prices, *Journal of Economic Dynamics and Control* 91, 59–82.

Belo, F, and X Lin, 2013, Labor Heterogeneity and Asset Prices: The Importance of Skilled Labor, Fisher College of Business Working Paper No. 2012-03-025.

Bentolila, S., and G. Bertola, 1990, Firing costs and labour demand: how bad is eurosclerosis?, *The Review of Economic Studies* 57, 381–402.

Bloom, Nicholas, 2009, The Impact of Uncertainty Shocks, *Econometrica* 77, 623–685.

———, Max Floetotto, Nir Jaimovich, Itay Saporta-Eksten, and Stephen Terry, 2012, Really uncertain business cycles, *NBER Working Paper* 18245.

Boguth, O., and L.A. Kuehn, 2009, Consumption volatility risk, in *EFA 2009 Bergen Meetings Paper*.

Bollerslev, T., G. Tauchen, and H. Zhou, 2009, Expected stock returns and variance risk premia, *Review of Financial Studies* 22, 4463–4492.

Bollerslev, T., L. Xu, and H. Zhou, 2012, Stock return and cash flow predictability: The role of volatility risk, *Available at SSRN 2177046*.

Button, P., 1990, The cost of labour turnover: an accounting perspective, *Labour Economics and Productivity* 2, 245–73.

Caballero, R.J., and E.M.R.A. Engel, 1993, Microeconomic adjustment hazards and aggregate dynamics, *The Quarterly Journal of Economics* 108, 359–383.

Caballero, Ricardo J, Eduardo M. R. A. Engel, and John Haltiwanger, 1997, Aggregate Employment Dynamics: Building From Microeconomic Evidence, *The American Economic Review* 87, 115–137.

Campbell, J Y, S Giglio, C Polk, and R Turley, 2012, An intertemporal CAPM with stochastic volatility, Manuscript.

Cascio, W.F., 1991, *Costing human resources* (South-Western Educational Publishing).

Chan, Louis K.C., Josef Lakonishok, and Theodore Sougiannis, 2001, The Stock Market Valuation of Research and Development Expenditures, *Journal of Finance* 56, 2431–2456.

Chen, Huafeng, Marcin Kacperczyk, and Hernan Ortiz-Molina, 2011, Labor unions, operating flexibility, and the cost of equity, *Journal of Financial and Quantitative Analysis* 46, 25–58.

Chow, C.S., and J.N. Tsitsiklis, 1991, An optimal one-way multigrid algorithm for discrete-time stochastic control, *Automatic Control, IEEE Transactions on* 36, 898–914.

Cohen, R.B., P.A. Gompers, and T. Vuolteenaho, 2002, Who underreacts to cash-flow news? evidence from trading between individuals and institutions, *Journal of Financial Economics* 66, 409–462.

Cooper, R., and J.L. Willis, 2009, The cost of labor adjustment: Inferences from the gap, *Review of Economic dynamics* 12, 632–647.

Danthine, Jean-Pierre, and John B. T3 Donaldson, 2002, Labour Relations and Asset Returns, *The Review of Economic Studies* 69, 41–64.

Dixit, A.K., 1993, *The art of smooth pasting* . vol. 2 (Routledge).

Dixit, Avinash, 1997, Investment and Employment Dynamics in the Short Run and the Long Run, *Oxford Economic Papers* 49, 1–20.

Dixit, Avinash Kamalakar, and Robert S. Pindyck, 1994, *Investment under uncertainty* (Princeton university press).

Dolfin, Sarah, 2006, An examination of firms' employment costs., *Applied Economics* 38, 861–878.

Donangelo, A., 2011, Labor mobility: Implications for asset pricing, Forthcoming, Journal of Finance.

Epstein, Larry G., and Stanley E. Zin, 1989, Substitution, risk aversion, and the temporal behavior of consumption and asset returns: A theoretical framework, *Econometrica* pp. 937–969.

Fairfield, P.M., J.S. Whisenant, and T.L. Yohn, 2003, Accrued earnings and growth: Implications for future profitability and market mispricing, *The Accounting Review* 78, 353–371.

Fama, E.F., and K.R. French, 1993, Common risk factors in the returns on stocks and bonds, *Journal of financial economics* 33, 3–56.

Fama, E.F., and K R French, 1997, Industry costs of equity, *Journal of Financial Economics* 43, 153–193.

Fama, E.F., and J.D. MacBeth, 1973, Risk, return, and equilibrium: Empirical tests, *The Journal of Political Economy* pp. 607–636.

Fama, Eugene F., and Kenneth R. French, 2008, Dissecting Anomalies, *Journal of Finance* 63, 1653–1678.

Fernández-Villaverde, Jesús, Pablo A Guerrón-Quintana, Keith Kuester, and Juan Rubio-Ramírez, 2011, Fiscal volatility shocks and economic activity, Discussion paper, National Bureau of Economic Research.

Fernández-Villaverde, Jesús, Pablo A Guerrón-Quintana, Juan Rubio-Ramirez, and Martin Uribe, 2009, Risk matters: The real effects of volatility shocks, Discussion paper, National Bureau of Economic Research.

Hamermesh, Daniel S., and Gerard A Pfann, 1996, Adjustment Costs in Factor Demand, *Journal of Economic Literature* 34, 1264–1292.

Haugen, R.A., and N.L. Baker, 1996, Commonality in the determinants of expected stock returns, *Journal of Financial Economics* 41, 401–439.

Hou, Kewei, and David T. Robinson, 2006, Industry Concentration and Average Stock Returns, *The Journal of Finance* 61, 1927–1956.

Jagannathan, Ravi, and Zhenyu Wang, 1998, An asymptotic theory for estimating beta-pricing models using cross-sectional regression, *The Journal of Finance* 53, 1285–1309.

Justiniano, Alejandro, and Giorgio E Primiceri, 2008, The time varying volatility of macroeconomic fluctuations, *American Economic Review* 98, 604–641.

Kandel, S, and R F Stambaugh, 1990, Expectations and volatility of consumption and asset returns, *Review of Financial Studies* 3, 207–232.

King, R.G., and S.T. Rebelo, 1999, Resuscitating real business cycles, *Handbook of macroeconomics* 1, 927–1007.

Kydland, F.E., 1984, Labor-force heterogeneity and the business cycle, in *Carnegie-Rochester Conference Series on Public Policy* vol. 21 pp. 173–208. Elsevier.

Lewellen, Jonathan, Stefan Nagel, and Jay Shanken, 2010, A skeptical appraisal of asset pricing tests, *Journal of Financial Economics* 96, 175–194.

Li, D, 2011, Financial Constraints, R&D Investment, and Stock Returns, *Review of Financial Studies* 24, 2974–3007.

Lin, Xiaoji, 2012, Endogenous technological progress and the cross-section of stock returns, *Journal of Financial Economics* 103, 411–427.

Matsa, David A, 2010, Capital Structure as a Strategic Variable: Evidence from Collective Bargaining, *The Journal of Finance* 65, 1197–1232.

Merchants and Manufacturers Association, 1980, *Turnover and Absenteeism Manual* (Merchants and Manufacturers Association).

Merz, Monika, and Eran Yashiv, 2007, Labor and the market value of the firm, *The American Economic Review* 97, 1419–1431.

Mincer, J., 1962, On-the-job training: Costs, returns, and some implications, *The Journal of Political Economy* pp. 50–79.

Novy-Marx, R, 2011, Operating Leverage, *Review of Finance* 15, 103–134.

Oi, Walter Y., 1962, Labor as a quasi-fixed factor, *Journal of Political Economy* 70, 538–555.

Parsons, Donald O., 1986, The employment relationship: Job attachment, work effort, and the nature of contracts, in Orley C Ashenfelter Layard, and Richard, ed.: *Handbook of Labor Economics* . pp. 789–848 T2 – (Elsevier).

Pfann, G A, and B Verspagen, 1989, The structure of adjustment costs for labour in the Dutch manufacturing sector, *Economics Letters* 29, 365–371.

Pratt, Ryan, 2011, A Structural Model of Human Capital and Leverage, .

Rosen, Sherwin, 1968, Short-Run Employment Variation on Class-I Railroads in the U.S., 1947-1963, *Econometrica* 36, 511–529.

Rouwenhorst, K. Geert, 1995, *Frontiers of business cycle research* . chap. Asset Pricing Implications of equilibrium business cycle models, pp. 294–330 (Princeton Univ Press).

Rust, J., 1996, Numerical dynamic programming in economics, *Handbook of computational economics* 1, 619–729.

Schmalz, Martin C., 2011, Managing Human Capital Risk, Manuscript.

Stokey, N.L., 2009, *The economics of inaction: Stochastic control models with fixed costs* (Princeton University Press).

Stokey, Nancy L, 2008, *The Economics of Inaction: Stochastic Control models with fixed costs* (Princeton University Press).

Titman, S., K.C. Wei, and F. Xie, 2004, Capital investments and stock returns, *Journal of Financial and Quantitative Analysis* 39, 677—700.

Weil, Philippe, 1990, Nonexpected utility in macroeconomics, *The Quarterly Journal of Economics* 105, 29–42.

Welch, Ivo, and Amit Goyal, 2008, A comprehensive look at the empirical performance of equity premium prediction, *Review of Financial Studies* 21, 1455–1508.

Wolak, Frank A., 1989, Testing inequality constraints in linear econometric models, *Journal of Econometrics* 41, 205–235.

Zhou, Hao, 2010, Variance risk premia, asset predictability puzzles, and macroeconomic uncertainty, Manuscript.

Figure 1
Optimal Employment Choice

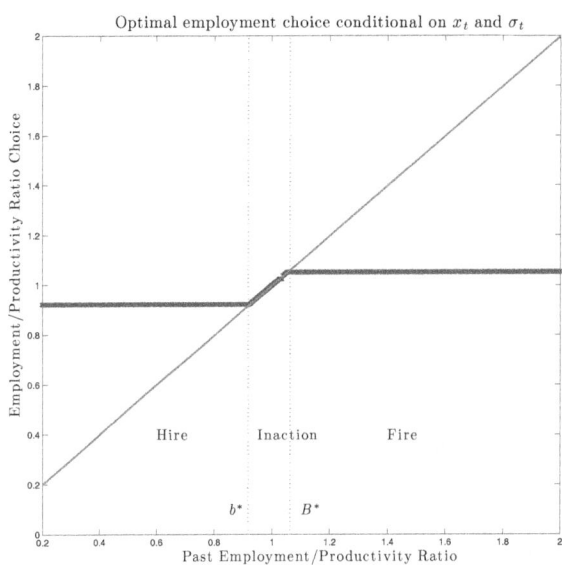

(a) Optimal employment choice

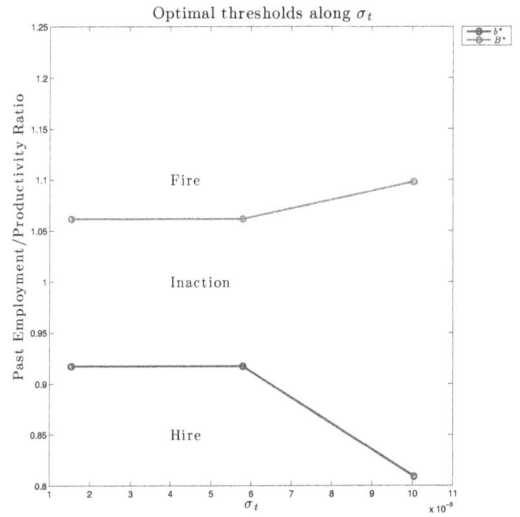

(b) Impact of uncertainty on the optimal inaction region

Panel (a) of Figure 1 displays the optimal choice of labor-aggregate productivity ratio $\tilde{n}_{i,t}$ along with the optimal inaction region $(b^*(\Delta a_t, \sigma_t), B^*(\Delta a_t, \sigma_t))$ for $(\Delta a_t, \sigma_t) = (0, \sigma_2)$. The labor-aggregate productivity ratio is defined as $\frac{n_{i,t}}{A_t^{1/(1-\alpha)}}$. Panel (b) displays the impact of aggregate uncertainty σ_t on the optimal inaction region $(b^*(\Delta a_t, \sigma_t), B^*(\Delta a_t, \sigma_t))$ for $\Delta a_t = 0$.

Figure 2
Model's Implications for The Cross-section of Expected Equity Returns

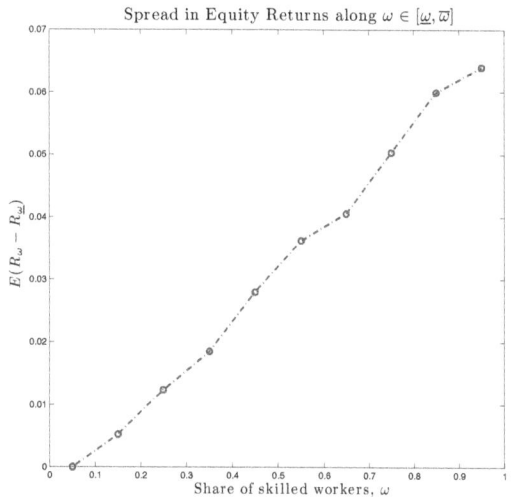

(a) Average equity returns in excess of the return on the firm with the lowest ω

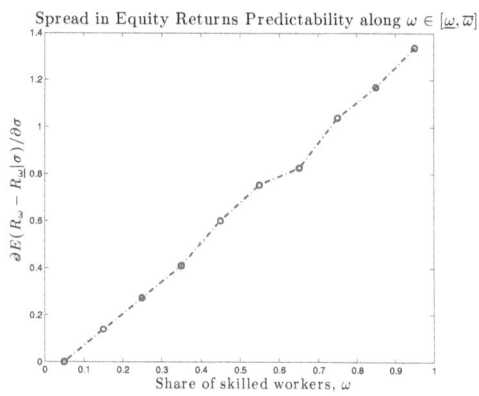

(b) Change in expected equity returns in excess of the return on the firm with the lowest ω when uncertainty increases one standard deviation

Panel (a) of Figure 2 displays the average equity returns on a firm with a share of skilled workers ω in excess of the return on the firm with the lowest ω, $E(R_\omega - R_{\underline{\omega}})$, for different values of ω. Panel (b) of Figure 2 displays the change in expected equity returns in excess of the return on the firm with the lowest ω when uncertainty increases one standard deviation, $\partial E(R_\omega - R_{\underline{\omega}}|\sigma_t)/\partial \sigma$.

Figure 3

Expected Equity Returns Under Alternative Investor's Preferences

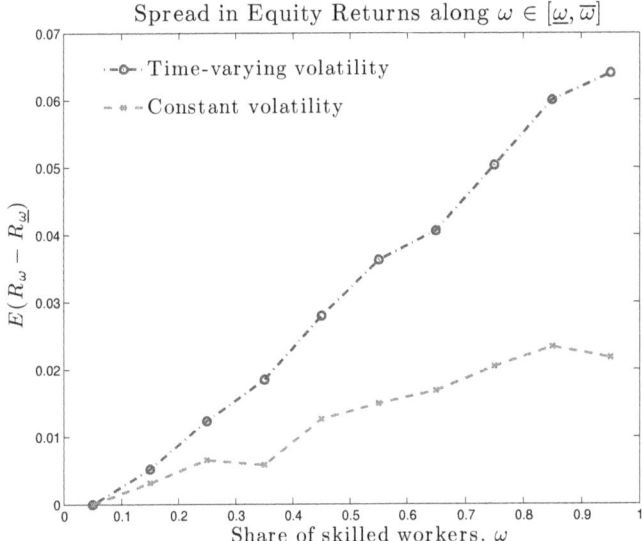

Figure 3 displays the expected equity return on a firm with a share of skilled workers ω in excess of the return on the firm with the lowest ω. The line with circular markers comes from the baseline model assuming time-varying aggregate volatility. The line with cross markers corresponds to the case in which aggregate volatility is constant.

Figure 4

Optimal Inaction Region Across Firms

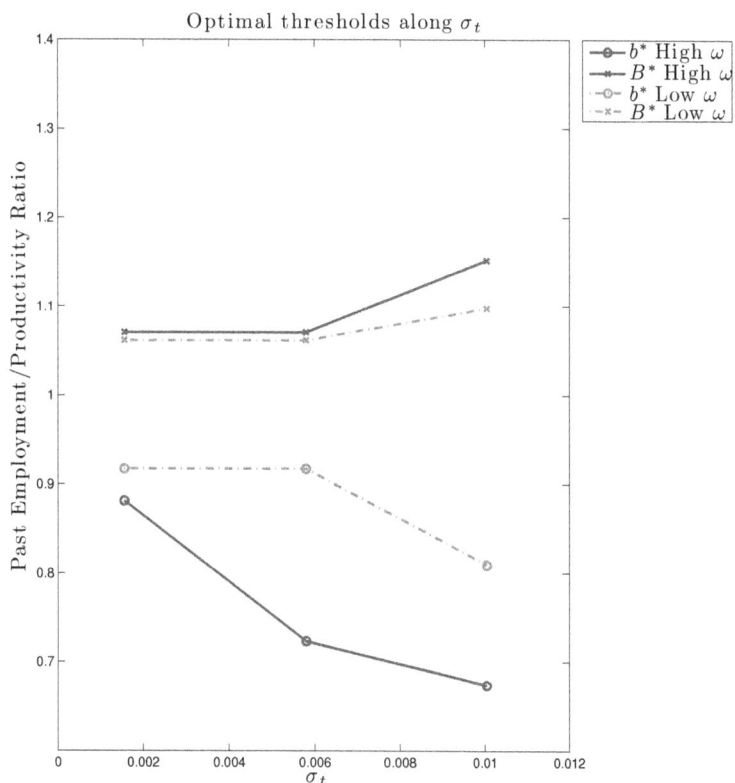

Figure 4 displays the optimal inaction region $(b^*(\Delta a_t, \sigma_t), B^*(\Delta a_t, \sigma_t))$ for a firm with a high share of low-skilled workers (low-ω) and one with a high share of high-skilled workers (high-ω).

Figure 5

Cross-Sectional Regression for 5 Reliance on Skilled Labor and 25 Size-Reliance on Skilled Labor Portfolios

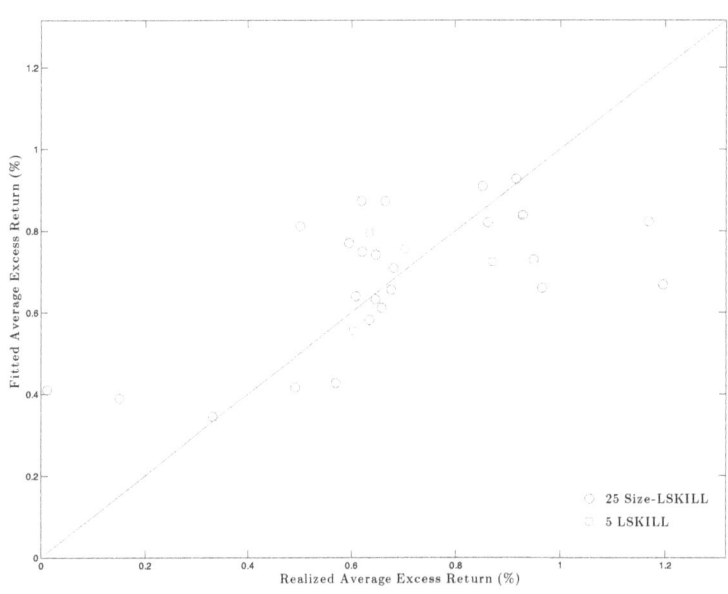

	λ_0	λ_{vrp}	R^2 % (GLS)
Coeff.	-0.908	-0.995	40.8 (40.5)
t-stat FM	(-1.324)	(-2.615)	
t-stat JW	(-1.113)	(-2.296)	

The scatter plot in Figure 5 displays the average equity returns in excess of the risk-free rate against the fitted expected equity excess returns for 5 portfolios sorted on the reliance on skilled labor and 25 portfolios sorted on size and reliance on skilled labor. The estimated value for the expected excess return comes from the following cross-sectional regression model,

$$\mathbb{E}(r_i) = \lambda_0 + \lambda_{vrp}\beta_{vrp,i} \tag{22}$$

The cross-sectional model coefficients are estimated as in Fama and MacBeth (1973), first I estimate $\beta_{vrp,i}$ as the slope coefficient of a time-series regression of excess returns on portfolio i, $r_{t,i}$, on a constant and the variance risk premium (VRP) defined as the difference between implied volatility and realized volatility as in Bollerslev, Tauchen, and Zhou (2009). In the second stage, I estimate the cross-sectional model using the estimated $\beta_{vrp,i}$. The table reports in parenthesis the estimated coefficients of the cross-sectional regression along with Fama and MacBeth (1973) and Jagannathan and Wang (1998) t-statistics. The table also reports the R^2 adjusted for degrees of freedom, and the generalized least squares (GLS) R^2 in parenthesis. The sample covers January 1990 to June 2011.

Table 1
Calibration

Parameter	Definition	Value	Source
β	Subjective discount factor	0.9989	Bansal, Kiku, and Yaron (2012)
γ	Risk aversion	10	Bansal, Kiku, and Yaron (2012)
ψ	Intertemporal elasticity of substitution	2	Bansal, Kiku, and Yaron (2012)
α	Labor share	2/3	U.S. Bureau of Labor Statistics
λ	Relative efficiency of skilled workers	2	
ζ	Worker's compensation parameter	2.88	Cooper and Willis (2009)
μ	Aggregate technology consumption	0.0015	Bansal, Kiku, and Yaron (2012)
ρ	Technology growth persistence	0.975	Bansal, Kiku, and Yaron (2012)
χ^1	Linear cost of adjusting skilled labor	6-months wage	Parsons (1986)
χ^2	Linear cost of adjusting unskilled labor	1/4-month wage	Cooper and Willis (2009)

Table 1 presents the benchmark parameter values used to solve and simulate the model which are calibrated at a monthly frequency.

Table 2
Labor Adjustment Costs Summary Statistics

Variable	No. obs.	Overall Mean	Std. Dev.	By education <12 yrs.	=>12 yrs.
Newly hired employee					
Age	3612	27.34	10.00	25.56	27.39
Relevant experience (months)	3437	45.53	67.76	36.19	46.09
Gender (Male=1)	3654	0.51	0.50	0.66	0.46
Time recruiting for position (days)	2487	18.07	37.30	12.05	19.48
No. of persons interviewed for position	3606	4.63	8.85	3.27	5.04
Hrs. spent training by employees & superiors	3473	32.82	37.06	27.98	34.79
Productivity gap	3568	15.69	18.82	12.73	16.84
Max wage for position US$/hour	2558	5.57	2.63	4.69	5.72
Size (hundreds of employees)	3661	0.73	2.25	0.53	0.78

Table 2 presents summary statistics of several personal characteristics of newly hired employees as well as the costs associated with the hiring process. The statistics are based on firm-level data from the 1980 Employer Opportunity Pilot Project (EOPP).

Table 3

Labor Adjustment Costs and the New Hire's Education

	Dependent Variable			
	Days recruiting	No. interviewed	Hrs. training	Productivity gap
Education (1=HS or more)	6.032***	1.439***	4.625***	3.089**
	(1.801)	(0.427)	(1.626)	(1.244)
Age	0.200*	-0.013	0.034	-0.047
	(0.120)	(0.025)	(0.093)	(0.050)
Experience	-0.007	0.000	-0.051***	-0.009
	(0.017)	(0.003)	(0.015)	(0.008)
Sex (1=male)	1.380	-1.046**	-0.289	-1.275
	(2.106)	(0.531)	(1.672)	(0.897)
Size	0.586	0.211	0.511	-0.249
	(0.497)	(0.150)	(0.405)	(0.188)
N	2287	3237	3145	3220

Table 3 presents the estimated coefficients from a regression of different costs associated with hiring a new employee on the level of education, age, gender, and relevant experience of the new hire, and the size of the establishment. The regressions also include unreported dummy variables to control fixed industry characteristics at the 3-digit SIC level. Education is a dummy variable equal to 1 when the newly hired has a high-school diploma or more education, experience is relevant job experience in months, sex is a dummy variable that equals to 1 if the newly hired is male, size is the number of workers in hundreds, and the last new hire productivity gap is the productivity of the last employee in the position minus the productivity of the new employee as reported by the manager. Standard errors clustered at the 3-digit SIC level are reported in parenthesis. The 1%, 5%, and 10% significance levels are denoted with ***, **, and *, respectively.

Table 4
Labor Adjustment Costs and the Position's Wage

	Dependent Variable			
	Days recruiting	No. interviewed	Hrs. training	Productivity gap
ln Wage	14.661***	1.970***	17.847***	5.293***
	(3.766)	(0.672)	(3.178)	(1.663)
Age	0.107	0.002	-0.021	-0.108
	(0.104)	(0.032)	(0.108)	(0.072)
Experience	-0.019	-0.003	-0.063***	-0.009
	(0.013)	(0.004)	(0.016)	(0.010)
Sex (1=male)	-3.857	-1.789***	-2.823	-2.958***
	(3.245)	(0.610)	(1.858)	(1.079)
Size	0.438	0.179	0.306	-0.311
	(0.496)	(0.160)	(0.413)	(0.212)
N	1669	2359	2291	2342

Table 4 presents the estimated coefficients from a regression of different costs associated with hiring a new employee on the top hourly wage for the position, the age, gender, and relevant experience of the new hire, and the size of the establishment. The regressions also include unreported dummy variables to control fixed industry characteristics at the 3-digit SIC level. Experience is relevant job experience in months, sex is a dummy variable that equals to 1 if the newly hired is male, size is the number of workers in hundreds, and the last new hire productivity gap is the productivity of the last employee in the position minus the productivity of the new employee as reported by the manager. Standard errors clustered at the 3-digit SIC level are reported in parenthesis. The 1%, 5%, and 10% significance levels are denoted with ***, **, and *, respectively.

Table 5
Reliance on Skilled Labor for Selected Industries

Industry	Reliance on Skilled Labor Index		
	1988-2010	1988-1999	2000-2010
Highest Reliance on Skilled Labor			
Engineering & architectural services	3.566	3.559	3.571
Legal services	3.562	3.599	3.532
Junior colleges	3.539	3.406	3.638
Testing laboratories	3.387	3.410	3.368
Offices of health practitioners	3.365	3.377	3.326
Guided missile & space vehicle manuf.	3.360	3.297	3.418
Gral. Medical & surgical hospitals	3.358	3.354	3.360
Offices & clinics of medical doctors	3.341	3.313	3.365
Computer & data processing services	3.288	3.450	3.152
Accounting services	3.274	3.355	3.233
Lowest Reliance on Skilled Labor			
Carpet & upholstery cleaning	1.738	1.684	1.783
Hotels & Motels	1.712	1.734	1.694
Video Tape & Disc Rental	1.709	1.773	1.661
Motor vehicle towing	1.671	1.682	1.614
Gasoline stations	1.655	1.810	1.281
Retail bakeries	1.625	1.738	1.573
Paperboard mills	1.571	1.516	1.673
Manufacturing man's & boy's suits & coats	1.549	1.423	1.665
Automobile parking	1.477	1.443	1.547
Eating places	1.467	1.372	1.563
Disinfecting & pet control services	1.357	1.368	1.347

Table 5 presents the reliance on skilled labor index for selected industries with the highest and lowest values of the index.

Table 6
Summary Statistics

Variable	Mean	Std. Dev.
Reliance on skilled labor (LSKILL)	2.633	0.450
log Book-to-Market equity (lnBM)	-0.638	0.879
log Market equity (lnME)	5.346	2.185
R&D intensity (R&D)	0.037	0.101
Operating leverage (OPLEV)	1.151	0.848
Earnings(+)/Assets (E/A+)	0.087	0.078
Investment rate (ASSETG)	0.135	0.344
Sales Beta (SALESB)	1.906	3.787
Labor Intensity (LABORINT)	0.011	0.038
Leverage (LEV)	0.356	0.226

Table 6 presents summary the sample mean and standard deviation of the variables used in the empirical section. The reliance on skilled labor index (LSKILL) is computed using the definition in (11), R&D intensity (R&D) is measured as R&D expenditures as a share of firm's market equity, operating leverage (OL) is measured as the ratio of operating costs to total assets value, profitability (E/A+) is measured as positive earnings before interest divided by total assets, assets growth (ASSETG) is defined as the annual growth in asset value, sales beta (SALESB) is measured as the slope coefficient from a regression of a firm's annual growth in sales on annual GDP growth using quarterly data, labor intensity (LABORINT) is defined as the ratio of number of employees to total assets value, and total leverage (LEV) is measured as the ratio of book liabilities (total assets minus book equity) to total market value of firm (market equity plus total assets minus book equity). The sample covers the period 1987–2011.

Table 7
Monthly Equity Returns and Reliance on Skilled Labor

	Dependent Variable: Monthly Equity Returns						
Explanatory Variable	(1)	(2)	(3)	(4)	(5)	(6)	(7)
LSKILL	0.248***	0.269***	0.280***	0.300***	0.301***	0.293***	0.291***
	(0.068)	(0.069)	(0.069)	(0.069)	(0.071)	(0.072)	(0.072)
lnBM	0.144***	0.155***	0.206***	0.141***	0.137***	0.137***	0.143***
	(0.032)	(0.032)	(0.036)	(0.036)	(0.036)	(0.036)	(0.038)
lnME	-0.156***	-0.145***	-0.151***	-0.153***	-0.155***	-0.155***	-0.155***
	(0.016)	(0.016)	(0.016)	(0.016)	(0.017)	(0.017)	(0.017)
R&D	2.905***	2.855***	2.844***	2.658***	2.668***	2.666***	2.680***
	(0.336)	(0.340)	(0.352)	(0.352)	(0.348)	(0.347)	(0.350)
OPLEV		0.131***	0.122***	0.072**	0.067**	0.074**	0.076**
		(0.032)	(0.031)	(0.030)	(0.031)	(0.031)	(0.030)
E/A+			1.818***	1.866***	1.842***	1.847***	1.787***
			(0.323)	(0.345)	(0.344)	(0.344)	(0.386)
ASSETG				-0.856***	-0.858***	-0.858***	-0.859***
				(0.062)	(0.062)	(0.062)	(0.062)
SALESB					0.020***	0.020***	0.020***
					(0.007)	(0.007)	(0.007)
LABORINT						-0.729***	-0.742***
						(0.261)	(0.262)
LEV							-0.066
							(0.161)
PASTRET	-0.022***	-0.022***	-0.022***	-0.023***	-0.023***	-0.023***	-0.023***
	(0.002)	(0.002)	(0.002)	(0.002)	(0.002)	(0.002)	(0.002)
$N \times T$	756,355	756,355	756,355	756,355	756,355	756,355	756,355

Table 7 presents the estimated coefficients from a regression of firm-level monthly stock returns on the reliance of skilled labor index (11), namely,

$$r_{ij,t+1} = \alpha + \beta_1 \text{LSKILL}_{j,t} + \mathbf{x}'_{ij,t}\gamma + u_{ij,t+1}$$

where r_{ij} is the monthly stock return of firm i from industry j in excess of the risk-free rate, and LSKILL_j is the reliance on skilled labor index at industry j. Industry membership j is defined by the firm's 3-digit SIC level and it is used to match the firm with its corresponding workers' skill index. The vector **x** includes controls for the (log) book-to-market equity ratio (lnBM), (log) market equity (lnME), past one-month excess returns (PASETRET), R&D intensity (R&D), profitability (E/A+), assets growth (ASSETG), sales beta (SALESB), labor intensity (LABORINT), and leverage (LEV). Regressions include unreported industry fixed-effects at the 1 digit SIC level and year fixed-effects, as well as dummy variables equal to one for firms reporting negative earnings, and zero R&D expenditures. Stock returns are monthly and expressed in percentage terms. The sample covers Jan-1987 to June-2011. Standard errors clustered at the 3-digit SIC are reported in parenthesis. The 1%, 5%, and 10% significance levels are denoted with ***, **, and *, respectively.

Table 8

Monthly Excess Returns on Portfolios Sorted on the Reliance on Skilled Labor

	Reliance on Skilled Labor Quintile							
	Q1 (Low)	Q2	Q3	Q4	Q5 (High)	Q5 - Q1	t-test	Wolak test
Equal-weighted	0.608	0.672	0.772	1.094	1.034	0.426	0.092	0.869
Value-weighted	0.592	0.627	0.683	0.935	0.838	0.246	0.214	0.780

Table 8 presents monthly excess returns on five portfolios sorted on the reliance on skilled labor index (LSKILL) along with the test for monotonicity proposed in Wolak (1989). Each year I sort firms according to their reliance on skilled labor into five portfolios and report the average monthly equity returns in excess of the risk-free rate for each quintile, as well as the difference between the the top and bottom quintiles. The last two columns report the p–value from the t-statistic testing the statistical difference between the quintile 5 and quintile 1, and the Wolak test. The Wolak (1989) test's null hypothesis is that a weakly monotonic relation exists between returns and the sorting variable. Excess returns are monthly and expressed in percentage terms. The sample covers July 1988 to June 2011.

Table 9
Reliance on Skilled Labor Premium and Aggregate Volatility

	Dependent Variable: Monthly Equity Returns			
Explanatory Variable	(1)	(2)	(3)	(4)
LSKILL × IVOL	0.303**		0.310**	
	(0.141)		(0.138)	
LSKILL × RVOL		0.232**		0.238**
		(0.103)		(0.101)
LSKILL	0.187**	0.116	0.237***	0.159**
	(0.072)	(0.079)	(0.077)	(0.081)
lnBM	0.290***	0.287***	0.266***	0.265***
	(0.036)	(0.036)	(0.040)	(0.041)
lnME	-0.121***	-0.106***	-0.122***	-0.104***
	(0.019)	(0.019)	(0.020)	(0.019)
R&D	3.672***	3.739***	3.297***	3.334***
	(0.337)	(0.341)	(0.349)	(0.352)
OPLEV			0.064**	0.064**
			(0.032)	(0.032)
E/A+			2.149***	2.020***
			(0.340)	(0.331)
ASSETG			-1.020***	-1.025***
			(0.058)	(0.060)
SALESB			0.023***	0.028***
			(0.007)	(0.007)
LABORINT			-1.178**	-1.439**
			(0.535)	(0.664)
LEV			0.101	0.063
			(0.160)	(0.162)

Table 9 presents the estimated coefficients from a regression of firm-level monthly stock returns on the on the reliance of skilled labor index LSKILL and its interaction with aggregate volatility σ, namely,

$$r_{ij,t+1} = \alpha + (\beta_1 + \beta_2 \sigma_t) \times \text{LSKILL}_{j,t} + \mathbf{x}'_{ij,t}\gamma + \beta_3 \sigma_t + u_{ij,t+1}$$

where r_{ij} is the monthly stock return of firm i from industry j in excess of the risk-free rate. Industry membership j is defined by the firm's 3-digit SIC level and it is used to match the firm with its corresponding workers' skill index. Aggregate volatility is approximated as the implied volatility computed using the VXO index based on S&P 100 index options (IVOL), and the realized volatility computed as the monthly standard deviation of the daily S&P 500 index (RVOL). Both measures are standardized. The vector $\mathbf{x}$ includes controls described in Table 7. The sample covers Jan-1987 to June-2011. Standard errors clustered at the 3-digit SIC are reported in parenthesis. The 1%, 5%, and 10% significance levels are denoted with ***, **, and *, respectively.

Table 10

Reliance on Skilled Labor Premium Aggregate Volatility: Time-Series Evidence

	Dependent Variable: LSKILL Risk Premium			
Explanatory Variable	EW	VW	EW	VW
IVOL	0.809**	0.717*		
	(0.400)	(0.390)		
VRP			0.284*	0.306*
			(0.171)	(0.165)
lnE/P	1.189	1.274	1.079	1.211
	(1.013)	(0.990)	(1.150)	(1.118)
INFL	-1.960**	-1.781**	-2.216**	-2.022**
	(0.875)	(0.842)	(0.898)	(0.860)
DFSP	-1.293	-1.215	-0.535	-0.577
	(1.111)	(1.069)	(0.973)	(0.931)
Constant	5.873**	5.831**	4.440	4.621
	(2.835)	(2.780)	(2.964)	(2.889)
Adj. R^2 (%)	3.18	2.90	2.53	2.87
T	275	275	257	257

Table 10 presents the estimated coefficients of the following time-series model,

$$rp_{t+1} = \alpha + \mathbf{x}'_t \beta + u_{t+1}$$

where rp_{t+1} is the risk compensation for a firm's the reliance on skilled labor (LSKILL), which I measure as the spread in returns between the top and bottom quintiles of portfolios sorted on LSKILL. The columns EW and VW use equal- and value-weighted returns, respectively. The vector $\mathbf{x}$ includes the earnings-price ratio lnE/P, the default spread defined as the difference between BAA and AAA-rated corporate bond yields, and inflation defined as the percentage change in the Consumer Price Index. The first two columns include implied volatility computed using the VXO index based on S&P 100 index options (IVOL), and the last tow columns include the variance risk premium (VRP) defined as the difference between implied volatility and realized volatility as in Bollerslev, Tauchen, and Zhou (2009). Both variables are standardized. The sample covers July 1988 to June 2011. For the estimates including the variance risk premium the sample covers January 1990 to June 2011. Newey-West standard errors are reported in parenthesis. The 1%, 5%, and 10% significance levels are denoted with ***, **, and *, respectively.

Table 11
Reliance on Skilled Labor Premium and Other Risk Factors

	Dep. Var.: LSKILL Risk Premium	
Explanatory Variable	EW	VW
MKT	0.062*	0.091**
	(0.036)	(0.042)
HML	-0.415***	-0.518***
	(0.054)	(0.068)
SMB	0.0898*	0.198***
	(0.052)	(0.062)
UMD	-0.007	-0.021
	(0.060)	(0.066)
Constant	0.399***	0.641***
	(0.152)	(0.187)
Adj. R^2 (%)	38.7	45.8
T	276	276

Table 11 presents the estimated coefficients from time-series regressions of the risk compensation for a firm's the reliance on skilled labor on excess market return (MKT), value (HML), size (SMB), and momentum (UMD) asset pricing factors. The columns EW and VW use the spread in returns between the top and bottom quintiles of portfolios sorted on LSKILL equal- and value-weighted, respectively. The sample covers July 1988 to June 2011. Newey-West standard errors are reported in parenthesis. The 1%, 5%, and 10% significance levels are denoted with ***, **, and *, respectively.

Table 12
Comparison of Cross-Sectional Regressions for 47 Industry Portfolios

	λ_0	λ_{lskill}	λ_{mkt}	λ_{hml}	λ_{smb}	R^2 % (GLS)
Coeff.	1.115	0.667	-0.522			36.6 (35.5)
t-stat FM	(3.527)	(1.782)	(-1.054)			
t-stat JW	(3.356)	(1.774)	(-0.916)			
Coeff.	0.555		0.193			0.1 (-0.1)
t-stat FM	(1.448)		(0.397)			
t-stat JW	(1.432)		(0.397)			
Coeff.	1.085		-0.236	-0.543	-0.198	22.1 (20.6)
t-stat FM	(3.778)		(-0.426)	(-1.590)	(-0.467)	
t-stat JW	(3.617)		(-0.416)	(-1.489)	(-0.454)	

Table 12 reports the estimated coefficients from three cross-sectional asset pricing models. The first model is the following,

$$\mathbb{E}(r_i) = \lambda_0 + \lambda_{lskill}\beta_{lskill,i} + \lambda_{mkt}\beta_{mkt,i} \quad (23)$$

The cross-sectional model coefficients are estimated as in Fama and MacBeth (1973), first I estimate $\beta_{lskill,i}$ as the slope coefficient of a time-series regression of excess returns on portfolio i, $r_{t,i}$, on a constant and the spread in returns between the top and bottom quintiles of portfolios sorted on LSKILL. Similarly, $\beta_{mkt,i}$ is the slope coefficient of a time-series regression of excess returns on portfolio i, $r_{t,i}$, on a constant and the excess return on the value-weighted CRSP index. The second model is the traditional CAPM, and the third model is the Fama and French (1993) three-factor model. Fama and MacBeth (1973) and Jagannathan and Wang (1998) t-statistics are reported in parenthesis. The table also reports the R^2 adjusted for degrees of freedom, and the generalized least squares (GLS) R^2 in parenthesis. The sample covers July 1988 to June 2011.